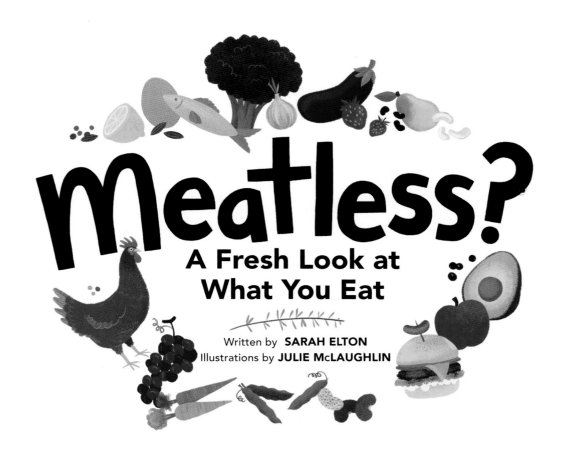

Meatless?

A Fresh Look at
What You Eat

Written by **SARAH ELTON**

Illustrations by **JULIE McLAUGHLIN**

Owlkids Books

For Anisa and Nadia whose dinner table questions about why we eat meat and the animals our food comes from always inspire me. — SE

For my family, Matt SB, Shannon, and always—Mr. Pants. — JM

Text © 2017 Sarah Elton
Illustrations © 2017 Julie McLaughlin

Owlkids Books acknowledges the financial support of the Canada Council for the Arts, the Ontario Arts Council, the Government of Canada through the Canada Book Fund (CBF) and the Government of Ontario through the Ontario Media Development Corporation's Book Initiative for our publishing activities.

Published in Canada by
Owlkids Books Inc.
10 Lower Spadina Avenue
Toronto, ON M5V 2Z2

Published in the United States by
Owlkids Books Inc.
1700 Fourth Street
Berkeley, CA 94710

Cataloguing data available from Library and Archives Canada

Library of Congress Control Number: 2016952838

ISBN 978-1-926818-43-6 (hardback)

Edited by: Niki Walker
Designed by: Alisa Baldwin and Danielle Arbour

ONTARIO ARTS COUNCIL
CONSEIL DES ARTS DE L'ONTARIO
an Ontario government agency
un organisme du gouvernement de l'Ontario

Canada Council
for the Arts
Conseil des Arts
du Canada

Canadä

Manufactured in Shenzhen, Guangdong, China, in December 2016, by WKT Co. Ltd.
Job #16CB1415

A   B   C   D   E   F

Publisher of Chirp, chickaDEE and OWL
www.owlkidsbooks.com

Owlkids Books is a division of  Bayard CANADA

CONTINTS

INTRODUCTDN:

The Day I Kiled
a Chicken

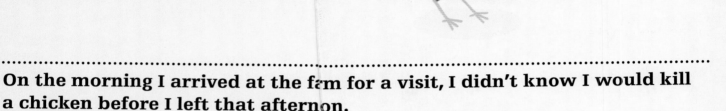

On the morning I arrived at the fam for a visit, I didn't know I would kill a chicken before I left that afternon.

I've eaten meat my whole life, but I'd never had to kill something that walked and squawked and breathed.

Ian, the farmer I was visiting, took me on a tour of the farm. We stopped by the barn, where the hens were hiding from the hot sun. He told me it was time to slaughter one of the old birds and asked if I wanted to help.

I said yes. It as a spur-of-the-moment desion. But I figured that if I eat meat, I should learn how a live chicken becomes dinner. Ian piked up a bird and told me to hod on to her feet. Tightly. He spred me the hard part and took he knife to her throat. Then he cut it, with my help steadyingher.

At that momen, when I watched a living being become food, I finally understood what it means to eat meat.

To eat meat, someone has to kill an animal. You are taking a life to support your own. This is something to think about. If you're reading this book, it's something you might have thought about already. And you wouldn't be the only one.

Humans have long struggled with the idea of eating another living being. Thousands of years ago, in countries like China, India, and Greece, people were questioning whether eating meat was wrong. And many religions throughout the ages have told people not to eat the flesh of living things.

Today, it can be easy to forget that meat is flesh. Most meat comes wrapped in plastic or packaged as chicken fingers or hot dogs or beef ravioli or chicken pad thai.

I am not a vegetarian. For my birthday every year, my grandmother used to make me chicken legs rolled in cornflakes. I still love a roasted chicken dinner, and chicken soup is my favorite. But there was something powerful about seeing a chicken die that made me look at the meat I eat in a new way.

It also made me more curious about people who choose not to eat it and their reasons why. I wanted to see meat from the point of view of those who've thought hard about it. What I learned is that the question of whether or not to eat meat is a whole lot more complicated—and interesting—than I ever imagined.

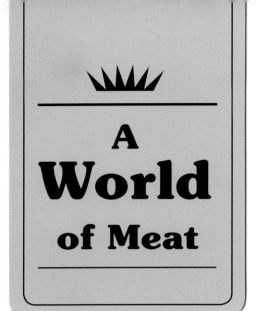

A World of Meat

These days, there's a lot of talk online, in books and magazines, and on TV about whether we should eat less meat.

One reason is because people today eat more meat than anyone in the history of humankind, and this raises questions for our health and the health of our environment. As little as fifty years ago, people ate a lot less meat than we do—a third less. That means for every three hamburgers we eat today, our grandparents would have eaten only two when they were growing up. Today, many North Americans eat meat at every meal. Bacon and sausage at breakfast, cold cuts at lunch, and chops at dinner.

And it's not just that meat-eaters are eating more meat. The love of meat is spreading quickly to countries like China and India, where people haven't traditionally eaten much meat—or any at all.

And since more people live in these two countries than in any other country in the world, demand for meat is growing.

WHAT MEAT DO YOU EAT?

The most common animals raised for food around the world are chickens, cows, sheep, pigs, and goats.

But lots of other animals are kept for food, including horses, camels, buffaloes, rabbits, and dogs. Birds such as quails, turkeys, and emus are raised for their meat. Fish, seafood, and reptiles, including snakes, are both farmed and caught in the wild. And plenty of people depend on meat from animals they hunt, like deer, moose, caribou, and wild birds like grouse and Canada geese.

The meat people choose to eat depends on their culture. Different cultures eat different foods—and different animals. One person's pet can be another person's dinner! The same goes for eating meat versus keeping a vegetarian diet. How you feel about what's on your plate can be influenced by many things, including where you live and how you were brought up.

A Tradition of Mainly Meat

Way up north in the Arctic, winter lasts many, many months. It's cold, and the land is covered with snow and ice for much of the year. Despite the freezing weather, people have lived all around the Arctic Circle for thousands of years.

In Canada's Arctic, the Inuit have long relied for nourishment on the meat and fish they hunt. Because no plants grow for most of the year, vegetables haven't traditionally been part of the Inuit diet—though in the short summer, wild berries and medicinal plants do get added to it. Today in the city of Iqaluit, if you were to ask people to name their favorite foods, many would say seal meat, caribou, and Arctic char. If you're Inuit, you call this "country food."

What Is a Vegetarian, Exactly?

A vegetarian is someone who chooses not to eat meat.

Although vegetarianism is thousands of years old, the word "vegetarian" wasn't used in English to describe this way of eating until the 1840s.

Since then, the word has become pretty common. There are vegetarian restaurants and vegetarian menus for school lunches. Candies, packaged foods, even shampoos and skin creams are often labeled as vegetarian when they are free of animal ingredients.

But only a small percentage of people are true vegetarians. In North America, fewer than five out of every hundred people

never eat meat. In Europe, the number is only slightly higher. The country with the most vegetarians is India, where about one-third of the people don't eat meat.

That said, more and more adults—and kids, too—are becoming vegetarians. And some people who do eat meat are deciding to have less of it. These changes have led to the invention of even more snappy new words like "semi-vegetarian," "flexitarian," and "vegivore." All these words describe someone who's cut most of the meat out of his or her diet but still eats some every now and then.

SO WHAT *DO* VEGETARIANS EAT?

Vegetarians can eat many different foods, like vegetables and fruit, nuts, seeds, and legumes. Legumes include foods such as lentils, beans, peas, and soybeans, which are high in protein.

Like meat-eaters, vegetarians also eat eggs and milk and honey. They eat bread and rice and pasta and all sorts of grains. What they don't eat is food made from the flesh of any animal—including fish. (And in case you were wondering, there is a name for someone who doesn't eat meat but does eat fish—pescatarian.)

People who are vegan go further, choosing to avoid any foods that come from animals, including eggs, honey, and dairy products.

The Father of Vegetarianism

Thousands of years ago, in ancient Greece, there was a philosopher named Pythagoras. (You might know him from math class. Pythagorean theorem is his big idea.) Pythagoras believed that animals and humans belong to the same family, and that when a human dies, the soul is reborn in the body of an animal. He set out dietary rules that included not eating meat. Today, he's sometimes called the Father of Vegetarianism.

PART ONE:

A History of
Meat-Eating

Before we talk about not eating meat, let's talk about why so many of us eat it in the first place.

Meat has been part of the human diet for thousands and thousands of years. Scientists and archaeologists can figure out what humans ate millennia ago by looking at the teeth in the oldest skeletons they've found. They also find clues in the fossilized garbage our ancestors left behind. Teeth marks and tool marks on old bones prove that people were biting and cutting into flesh, giving us clues to when humans started to eat meat.

Our early ancestors lived as hunter-gatherers. Instead of growing food, they collected it from nearby forests, grasslands, oceans, rivers, and lakes. They picked things that grew wild, like plants, mushrooms, berries, and roots. They hunted and caught wild animals, birds, and seafood. Instead of rice with chicken, or pasta with tomato sauce, their dinner might have been wild mushrooms, roots, and crayfish stew, or deer meat with berries.

I EAT MEAT, THEREFORE I AM?

Anthropologists who study how humans have evolved over thousands of years believe that meat has played a part in shaping who we are today. For one thing, all the nutrients in meat helped our brains to grow bigger—and therefore made us smarter. Anthropologists also think that hunting helped us develop language. That's because when our ancestors were hunting, they needed ways to communicate. Language allowed them to work together to track and catch a deer hiding in the bushes up ahead, for instance. Early human ancestors were eating animals 25 million years ago, so there's been a lot of time for hunting and meat-eating to make us … well, human.

LIVESTOCK = LIFE

Starting between 15,000 and 10,000 years ago, many human societies stopped hunting and gathering and instead started growing crops and keeping animals for food. Still, life for our ancestors was much different than it is for most of us today. There were no supermarkets. There weren't frozen foods or cans of soup or boxes of cereal. Everything had to be made from scratch. Even flour to make bread would have had to be ground from grain first. Producing and preparing food took up the majority of people's time. Kids didn't go to school. Instead, they helped grow, collect, and prepare enough food to feed the family.

A Ticket to Survival

Life was probably pretty hard when humans were first figuring out how to farm more than 10,000 years ago.

If a pest, disease, or bad weather destroyed the food crops or if animals got sick and died, people often starved. Sometimes they died. Much of day-to-day life was focused on growing enough food for the whole year and then figuring out how to make that food last. (In parts of the world, this is still the case for some families.)

During this time in history, humans didn't eat a lot of meat. With farms to tend, they could hunt only so often. And small farms could raise only so many animals. The animals that farmers did keep, however, were key to their survival.

Animals meant security. They helped to guard against starvation. If you had a chicken, you could eat eggs. If you had a cow, goat, or sheep, you could have milk. If you had male and female animals that could reproduce, you would have baby animals the next year. And once in a while, you could also eat nourishing meat.

More Than Meat

When we talk about how humans have long depended on animals for food, we can't forget that many cultures use more than just the meat.

In India and elsewhere, there is a tradition of using milk from cows and buffaloes. You don't have to kill these animals to draw their milk, which is made into all kinds of dairy products. Milk becomes yogurt. Cream becomes butter, which can be cooked and turned into clarified butter called ghee. Ghee lasts a long time without refrigeration. And big vats of milk are boiled and boiled to make delicious treats, including sweet fudge-like burfi and soft creamy balls of rasgulla that are soaked in syrup.

The Masai people of Kenya and the Berbers of North Africa have a long tradition of drawing blood from their live animals to drink.

In Ireland and many other countries, there are traditional foods made with blood. Blood sausage is one. It looks like any other sausage, but when you take a bite, the texture is softer. In the past, people used to make a small cut in a cow to collect the blood and then added it to their dishes. They would care for the wounds they made in the cow's skin so the animal could continue to live its normal life.

13

The Meaning of Meat

Throughout the history of human society, we've had deep beliefs about meat and what it means to us.

These beliefs have helped shape some of the values and ideas we still hold about meat today.

IN THE WEST, MEAT MEANT MONEY

During the Middle Ages in Europe, only the powerful people who ruled the land had access to large herds of cattle and sheep. No one but the lords and their friends were allowed to go hunting on their big estates. The rich kept this land for themselves. If the poor trespassed, they'd be in trouble. Although some well-to-do peasants had livestock, most people were poor peasants with few or no animals.

For centuries, kings, emperors, and nobles in Western countries showed off their wealth with feasts featuring meat. They served meat to impress their guests, as the wealthy and powerful were often the only people with access to it. To this day, meat remains a symbol of wealth in many parts of the world.

IN THE EAST, MEAT MEANT MODERATION

In China, the story of money and meat is a little different. Meat was traditionally out of reach for the average person, but even the rich did not eat much of it.

That's because vegetables and grains—not meat—were considered to be the foundation of healthy eating. One of the oldest Chinese texts that we know of describes some food rules.

14

It warns against eating too much meat. It says that after your meal, your breath should smell of rice, not meat.

For thousands of years in India, many people—both rich and poor—chose not to eat meat because they felt it was wrong to eat animals. In fact, when English travelers journeyed to India in the 1700s, they were shocked to find animal hospitals and other signs of humans treating animals as more than a source of food.

There's one story of an Indian emperor named Ashoka the Great. Around 265 BCE, Ashoka ruled over a vast land. One year, he sent his troops out to conquer more territory, and his soldiers killed many people. The amount of bloodshed horrified Ashoka. He swore he'd never again cause any violence—and that included killing animals to eat. Ashoka the Great converted to the Buddhist religion and became vegetarian. At his royal banquets, people were served rice and vegetables, fruit, yogurt, and sweet cakes. But never meat.

So in the past—like today— people thought about what it meant to eat meat. They made a choice about how much to eat based on their own beliefs and what kinds of food they had access to.

Religious **Rules**

Different religions have different rules that guide the way people eat. Religious laws combined with cultural traditions have long told people what animals they can and can't consume.

BUDDHISM

In Asia, between the sixth and fourth centuries BCE, a prince named Gautama was saddened by the suffering he saw around him. He believed that this misery could be lifted if people became more compassionate (that is, mindful of each other and all living things). Gautama became the founder of the Buddhist religion, which is followed today by hundreds of millions of people. Many Buddhists choose not to eat meat to avoid causing violence against other living beings.

JAINISM

In the Jain religion, it is believed that humans should never harm any living thing. Observant Jains not only avoid eating meat but they may also choose not to eat vegetables that come from the ground, like potatoes and carrots. This is in part because when you eat a carrot, you are eating its root, and that means you've killed the plant.

HINDUISM

Hinduism is a set of ancient beliefs and practices that has shaped people's eating habits for thousands of years, particularly in India. For some, non-violence, or *ahimsa*, is part of Hinduism. They believe that to observe ahimsa is to stop supporting violence, including the killing of animals. Another important part of Hindu philosophy for some is reincarnation, the belief that when you die, your soul can be reborn in the body of another being, including that of an animal.

ISLAM

Meat-eating is allowed in Islam, but pork is forbidden. The religion also has rules about how animals should be slaughtered so that the meat can be considered halal—which means prepared following religious law—and suitable to eat.

CHRISTIANITY

The Old Testament, which is sacred to both Christians and Jews, describes Adam and Eve living in the Garden of Eden, where they weren't allowed to eat meat. Only later did God permit humans to eat meat— but only certain types. Pork and shellfish were not allowed. The New Testament removed those restrictions, so there is no general rule about meat in Christianity today. Sometimes people do give it up though, such as during Lent, when some Catholics in particular avoid eating meat.

JUDAISM

People who follow the Jewish rules around food are said to keep kosher. For meat to be considered kosher, animals must be slaughtered in a certain way. While kosher rules don't specify a vegetarian diet, they do forbid eating some meats, like pork and shellfish.

PART TWO:

Why Go
Vegetarian?

A flight attendant makes his way down the aisle asking each passenger a revealing question: "Will you have chicken or beef?"

His words sum up just how important meat is to North American culture. He doesn't ask about salad, or offer a choice between rice and potatoes. All that matters is the meat.

So why do some people go against the mainstream and choose not to eat meat? It's a personal decision. Everyone has his or her own reasons. We've already seen that it can be because of a person's religious beliefs. Other reasons include health or environmental concerns.

To raise the millions and millions of animals needed to feed the billions of meat-eaters around the world, farms are getting bigger. And that means the problems connected to raising meat are growing, too. Farming animals uses a lot of natural resources, like water and land, and it can create a lot of pollution and greenhouse gases, too. So people worry about climate change and other effects that eating meat can have on the planet. Others believe the resources used to raise livestock would be put to better use

growing plants to feed people directly. Some are concerned about how animals are treated on these giant farms.

As people think about ways to fix these problems, they may wonder if skipping meat could help. Let's jump in and explore some of these issues more deeply.

Meatless
Mondays

You can help reduce greenhouse gases—and climate change—by making a small change to your weekly menu. That's the idea behind a campaign called Meatless Mondays that asks people to skip eating meat one day a week. It's a way of letting meat-eaters find out for themselves that they don't need meat every day. And the campaign spreads the idea that you can make a difference by simply choosing different foods.

19

Animal
Welfare

Cows, pigs, chickens, and ducks. You'll find all these animals on the happy farms of nursery rhymes and storybooks. But animal rights activists remind us that the big farms (where most of our meat is raised) don't look anything like those charming places.

FACTORY FARMING

Big farms, sometimes called factory or industrial farms, are usually home to only one type of animal—but lots of them. These farms raise as many animals as they can, as quickly as they can. For example, cattle are often grouped together on a type of farm called a feedlot. There can be tens of thousands of cows on the same farm. The cattle are fattened up until they reach what's called market weight—the right size to sell for butchering.

Similarly, chickens are raised in enormous barns called batteries, which can house as many as 100,000 birds. Pigs live in hog barns, where there can be tens of thousands of them under one roof. We raise so many animals this way that in Canada, alone, more than 20 million pigs are killed each year.

Many people are concerned with how animals are handled on these big farms, often packed in pens so small the livestock can barely move. Animal rights groups like People for the Ethical Treatment of Animals (PETA) note that the animals we raise for food are not treated nearly as well as those we choose as pets.

Organizations like the World Food Organization and Centers for Disease Control and Prevention have raised concerns about animal abuse, sickness, and air quality on industrial farms.

Of course, not all farms treat their animals poorly. Still, animal rights activists who promote vegetarianism argue that it doesn't matter how well a farmer treats livestock—the animals still die for us to eat.

Animals Have
Feelings, Too

When a creature can feel and think and smell and taste, it's called a sentient being. Humans are sentient. We feel things. Cats and dogs are also sentient beings. So are pigs, cows, sheep, chickens, and the rest of the animals we eat. Like humans, animals strive to live a life that is comfortable and free from pain. Scientists who study animals have found that even fish will choose to avoid being hurt if they can. This is why some people believe it is cruel to keep animals on farms, just to kill them for food, when we could eat other things instead.

The High Cost of Meat

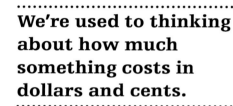

We're used to thinking about how much something costs in dollars and cents.

But the things we buy have another price—the environmental cost. That's the total impact that producing any item has on the environment. When it comes to meat, the environmental cost includes factors like whether forests have to be cleared to make room for livestock, how much waste and pollution are created to raise the animal and get it to your plate, and what ends up in the garbage when you're finished dinner.

MEAT'S BIG FEET

One way of measuring the environmental cost of a food is to calculate its environmental footprint by adding up all the land, water, and other resources needed to produce it and to absorb the waste. So to calculate the environmental footprint of, say, a hamburger you would include:

- the water and fertilizer used to grow food for the cow

- the fossil fuels needed to run tractors and other machinery on the farm

- how much food and water the cow ate and drank

- how much the cow pooped, and what happened to the poop

- the diesel that powered the truck that brought the cow to the slaughterhouse

- the energy used to process the meat and keep it refrigerated

- all the resources used to get the hamburger to the store and then onto your plate

A COW'S GOTTA EAT

It takes a lot more resources and creates more waste to make a pound of beef than it does a pound of beans. Why? Plants get their energy to grow directly from the sun, while livestock has to eat plants to grow. To fatten up the cows we eat as beef, we must *first* grow the feed crops that they eat, such as corn. That's why most meat today has a higher environmental cost than vegetables and grains.

Meat-Making Math

When people are thinking about the environmental cost of meat, they consider how much an animal needs to eat before it grows big enough to slaughter. One calculation they use is called the feed conversion ratio. It's a way of figuring out how much feed an animal needs to eat in order to turn that feed into meat. And not all meat is created equal.

To raise a chicken until it is big enough to be eaten, you need a lot less feed than you do to raise larger animals. A chicken only has to eat 1.65 kilograms/1.65 pounds of feed to make 1 kilogram/1 pound of meat—a ratio of 1.65:1. A cow, on the other hand, has to eat 10 kilograms/10 pounds of feed to produce 1 kilogram/1 pound of beef—a ratio of 10:1.

Greenhouse Gases

When you think about greenhouse gases and climate change, what comes to mind?

Clogged highways with thousands of cars spewing carbon dioxide in their exhaust? Factory smokestacks belching clouds of greenhouse gases? Thick, juicy steaks sizzling on a grill? Wait, what?

It's true. Everything you put in your mouth comes with a greenhouse gas price tag, whether it's an apple, a chocolate bar, or a hamburger. Growing and processing food takes energy and creates greenhouse gases, but some foods produce more greenhouse gases than others.

The table on the right shows some of our basic food sources and how much carbon dioxide is created to produce one kilogram/one pound of each.

FOOD SOURCE

LAMB

BEEF

CHEESE

PORK

CHICKEN

CANNED TUNA

NUTS

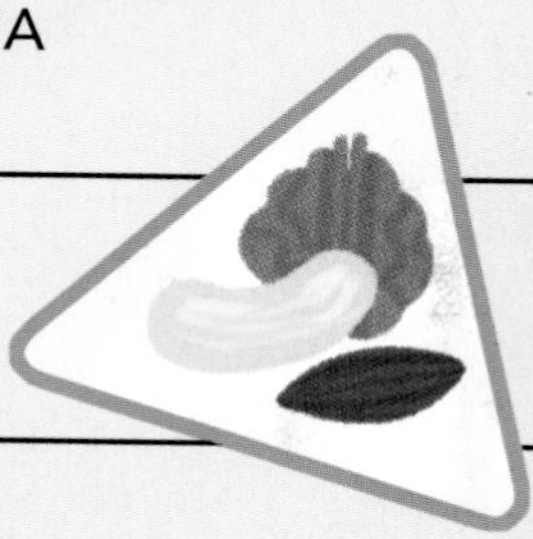

TOFU

DRY BEANS

LENTILS

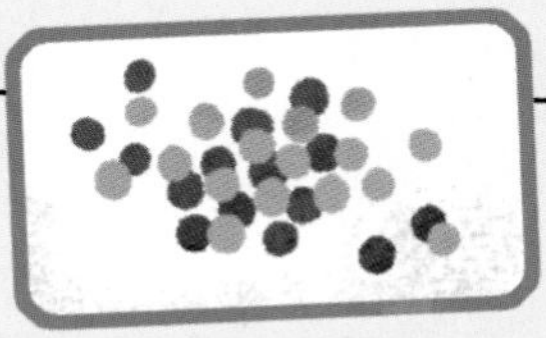

Kilograms/pounds of CO_2 generated for every kilogram/pound of food produced
39.3 KG/86.6 LBS
27 KG/59.5 LBS
13.5 KG/29.8 LBS
12.1 KG/26.7 LBS
6.9 KG/15.2 LBS
6.1 KG/13.4 LBS
2.3 KG/5.1 LBS
2.0 KG/4.4 LBS
2.0 KG/4.4 LBS
0.9 KG/2.0 LBS

errrrrp!

GASSY ANIMALS

The United Nations has asked people to eat less meat and dairy—or none at all—because it would be better for the planet. It turns out that 14.5 percent of greenhouse gas emissions are caused by meat and dairy production—that's more than comes from driving cars.

How does meat contribute to greenhouse gases? Cows, sheep, and goats belong to a class of animals called ruminants. They can digest something we can't: the cellulose in grasses. When ruminants digest cellulose, their stomachs produce methane, a greenhouse gas that the animals then belch out.

There's more. When animals eat, they also poop. If this waste isn't treated properly, it releases even more greenhouse gases. Add to that all the carbon dioxide released by machinery and trucks while getting meat from the farm to your plate, and you can see why meat has such a high greenhouse gas price tag.

Test-Tube Meat

Some people are working on how to produce meat without having to raise a real living, eating, breathing, gas- and waste-producing animal. Yes, that's right. They are growing meat from animal cells in a laboratory in an effort to bring down the environmental cost of meat-eating. Some say the test-tube meat tastes great. Others say they'd prefer to go vegetarian!

Enough Food for Everyone

A big question a lot of people are asking today is whether we can keep using the same farming methods to feed our growing population. And even if we think those methods can feed everyone, we also have to think about whether they're sustainable. In other words, can we keep farming the way we do now without running out of resources or ruining the planet in the process—and making it even harder for people to eat in the future?

These questions are particularly important when it comes to meat. Farmers are raising more and more animals—so many, in fact, that today 80 percent of the world's farmland is used for raising livestock.

MMMM, CRICKETS

Experts believe that by the year 2050, we will have to produce twice as much meat as we do today to keep up with rising demand from a growing population. Some scientists are now saying that if we want to feed the world in a way that doesn't harm the environment too much, more of us will need to eat insects. That's because insects have a much smaller environmental footprint than cows, chickens, pigs, and other livestock. They need less food and water and produce less waste.

Insects for dinner isn't a new idea. In fact, almost 2 billion people already include insects in their diets. In many cultures, bugs make healthy—and tasty!—snacks and meals. For instance, you can buy fried bamboo worms at food carts in Bangkok, Thailand, and caterpillars called *cuchamás* in central Mexico. Did you know that toasted crickets taste like pumpkin seeds and are quite delicious?

Some people have already started cricket farms because they expect bugs will one day be a hot commodity in countries where people don't eat them yet.

Food Security

While some people are eating lots of meat, many others are left out—particularly people in developing countries, many of whom don't have much money or many resources. Millions of people don't get enough nutritious food and often suffer from micronutrient deficiency. Even though these people aren't necessarily starving, they aren't getting enough healthy food to fuel their bodies properly. Having enough affordable, nutritious food is called food security.

Livestock raised in the United States eats seven times more grain than all Americans put together. Some people argue that the farmland used to raise this grain would be put to better use growing crops like legumes, which are highly nutritious and would feed people directly. Although enough food is produced to feed everyone today, making this change could lead to better food security now and in the future.

PART THREE:

If Not Meat, Then What?

Our bodies need all sorts of nutrients in order to grow and stay healthy.

Meat provides easy access to many of these nutrients. So vegetarians have to do a bit of planning when it comes to their food choices to be sure they are getting the nutrients they need from foods other than meat.

PROTEIN	MINERALS—IRON	MINERALS—ZINC
WHERE YOU'LL FIND IT: In your muscles and hair.	**WHERE YOU'LL FIND IT:** In your red blood cells (called hemoglobin) and in your muscle tissue.	**WHERE YOU'LL FIND IT:** In your cells.
WHAT IT DOES: Protein provides essential amino acids—essential because your body can get them only from food and must have them to function. Amino acids are also important for making hormones and repairing damaged tissues.	**WHAT IT DOES:** Iron helps your body make blood, which moves the oxygen you breathe into your lungs out to all the other tissues of your body.	**WHAT IT DOES:** Zinc helps your immune system work properly. It also helps your senses—like smell and taste—function.
MEAT-FREE SOURCES: Nuts, cheese, and legumes like lentils and beans.	**MEAT-FREE SOURCES:** Dried beans, peas, and lentils.	**MEAT-FREE SOURCES:** Flaxseed and soybean oils.

MINERALS—CALCIUM	FATS AND FATTY ACIDS	VITAMINS—B$_{12}$
WHERE YOU'LL FIND IT: In your bones.	**WHERE YOU'LL FIND THEM:** In your blood and stored in cells.	**WHERE YOU'LL FIND IT:** In nerve cells and blood cells.
WHAT IT DOES: Calcium builds strong bones and teeth.	**WHAT THEY DO:** Your body needs a few different kinds of fats and fatty acids—such as cholesterol and triglycerides—to work. Your body uses fat as fuel and to make hormones.	**WHAT IT DOES:** B$_{12}$ helps keep your brain and nerves healthy and teams up with iron to make new red blood cells.
MEAT-FREE SOURCES: Dried beans, broccoli, collard greens, and dairy products such as milk and yogurt.	**MEAT-FREE SOURCES:** Eggs, butter, flaxseed, coconut oil, nuts, and avocados.	**MEAT-FREE SOURCES:** Cheese, eggs, vitamin pills, foods fortified with vitamin B$_{12}$. Foods from plants don't naturally contain B$_{12}$.

29

Plant Power

When our ancestors switched from hunting and gathering to growing crops and keeping animals, they made an important discovery.

They figured out that if they ate a legume like a lentil, bean, or chickpea together with a grain like rice, wheat, or corn, their bodies would be healthy and strong—even without meat.

That's because combining a legume with a grain creates a complete protein. A complete protein is one that has all twelve essential amino acids.

Early farmers combined the legumes and grains that thrived where they lived. In Asia, that was rice and soybeans. In the Middle East, it was chickpeas, lentils, and wheat. In the Americas, corn and beans. In the Indian subcontinent, rice and lentils. In Europe, beans and wheat. Over time, cooks in different parts of the world came up with distinctive dishes based on these local ingredients.

A WORLD OF OPTIONS

If you choose not to eat meat, it is important for you to eat food combinations that give you complete proteins. Here are just a few of the many traditional dishes from around the world that feature this powerful combination of legume plus grain.

EMPANADA

Corn is soaked in limewater (as in calcium hydroxide, not the fruit) to release its nutrients, and then ground into flour and made into dough. Then the dough is stuffed with beans and turned into a complete protein in the shape of an empanada.

GALLO PINTO

In Latin American countries such as Nicaragua, white rice and black or red beans are cooked together to make a spotted dish. Some say it brings to mind a speckled rooster—that's what *gallo pinto* means in Spanish.

RIBOLLITA

This hearty Italian soup combines vegetables, beans, and stale wheat bread that is soaked in broth until soft. It's a style of Italian cooking called *cucina povera*, or peasant's kitchen, which uses up leftovers and also delivers a nutritious punch.

CHICKPEA COUSCOUS

Moroccan cuisine is known for its couscous, tiny pearls of wheat dough that are steamed until soft and fluffy. Serving couscous with a tagine stew made from chickpeas creates a complete protein by combining the grain with a legume.

DAL AND RICE

The lentil curry known as dal is a staple in countries such as Nepal, Bangladesh, India, and Pakistan. There are as many versions of dal as there are cooks, but these curries all provide the twelve essential amino acids—as long as you eat them with rice or flatbreads.

CONGEE AND TOFU SKINS

In Chinese cuisine, the simple rice porridge known as congee is enriched with tofu skins. Tofu is made from soybeans that are first ground to make a milk. When this milk is heated, a thick skin forms on top. Tofu skins are often sold dried, and they taste delicious.

Faux Meat— Bon Appétit!

Meat can give meals a delicious depth of flavor. But cooks figured out long ago that you don't have to hold back on taste when you choose not to put meat in your dish. Inventive people have discovered all sorts of creative ways to deliver meat's smoky or salty or just downright meaty taste. (They've even nailed the chewy-but-not-too-chewy texture.)

TOFU

Silky smooth or firm and chewy. Sweet and fresh or stinky as blue cheese. Tofu can be smoked, fermented, and aged to create all sorts of tastes, smells, and textures. But it all starts with a milky liquid made from soybeans, turned into a gelatin-like mass, then pressed. Tofu is likely as old as agriculture itself.

SEITAN

For centuries, Chinese cooks have been making a type of dough called seitan from wheat flour and water. If this dough is handled in a certain way, it takes on a texture that some say reminds them of meat—it's chewy in a good way. And depending on how the cook cuts it, seitan can look like duck or goose meat, chicken, pork, beef, or even seafood.

CASHEW CREAM AND NOUVEAU VEGGIE CUISINE

Chefs who cook vegan foods (made without any animal products) have dreamed up recipes like cashew cream to replace cream or cheese. This rich, creamy spread is made soaking cashew nuts in water and then puréeing them until they are smooth.

TEMPEH

You could call tempeh "soybean cheese." That's because, like cheese, tempeh is made through fermentation, a process in which yeast, bacteria, or mold digests the sugar that's naturally in the food. To make tempeh, you infect soybeans with a mold, press them into a square, and wait for them to ferment. The tempeh needs to sit for about two days to reach the perfect earthy, nutty taste. It's an ancient recipe that was invented on the Indonesian island of Java.

CHICKPEA FLOUR

Chickpeas are a type of legume that have been used in countless imaginative ways. In the south of France, chickpeas are ground into flour to make socca, a type of pancake. Take that same flour, mix it with water, add onions and spices, and you end up with a South Asian–style batter to deep-fry and turn into pakoras. Or you can mix water with the flour and simmer until your mixture is glossy. Pour this into a bowl to cool, and you'll have a tofu-like dish that's popular in Burma!

PART FOUR:

Becoming a
Vegetarian

If you're reading this book, there's a chance that you're thinking about becoming a vegetarian.

Or maybe you're thinking of cutting down on the amount of meat you eat. No matter what you are considering, here are some practical matters to think about.

WHERE TO START?

A good way to decide whether vegetarianism is for you is to do a trial run. Consider cutting meat out of your diet for a week or two. Talk about it with your family first. Together, research your food options and make a meal plan. Then see how it goes.

Try the same thing if you're thinking of being a flexitarian. Make sure you do your research and your planning with your family. Eat a healthy diet. And see what happens!

HOW DO YOU MAKE SURE YOU HAVE A HEALTHY DIET?

1. SEE TO IT THAT YOU'RE EATING ENOUGH PROTEIN
and all the other nutrients your body once got from meat (see pages 28-29). Research easy ways to include nuts, seeds, legumes, and colorful fruits and vegetables in your meals.

2. SUBSTITUTE CHEESE FOR MEAT.
Instead of meat-filled lasagna, go for cheese lasagna. Rather than a ham sandwich, have a cheese sandwich. But don't just rely on this swap. As tasty as cheese can be, your diet needs to be more varied.

3. BE WARY OF PROCESSED MEAT SUBSTITUTES
like vegetarian ground beef, vegetarian bacon, and vegetarian chicken fingers. They're typically packed with salt and all sorts of preservatives, so these should be eaten in moderation.

4. LEARN TRICKS TO IMITATE THE TEXTURE OF MEAT WITHOUT USING PROCESSED SUBSTITUTES.
Rather than adding fake ground beef to your pasta sauce, use a plain, firm tofu that has no added ingredients. Try crumbling some into a tomato sauce to spoon over spaghetti. Or cube it and add it to curries and stir-fries.

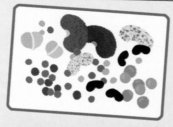

5. DON'T FORGET THOSE LEGUMES.
They are super nutritious, and a package of dried lentils or beans costs a fraction of what you'd pay for meat. Legumes come in a variety of shapes, sizes, and colors. They can be cooked into so many dishes and in so many different styles, you'll never get bored. Think curries, veggie burgers, salads, stews, and more.

6. LEARN TO COOK FROM SCRATCH!
Becoming a vegetarian is a great opportunity to pick up a new skill that will serve you for the rest of your life—even if you decide to eat meat again one day. Cooking from scratch helps you avoid all the added sugar, salt, preservatives, and other unhealthy ingredients that are often added to processed foods.

A Meat-Free Week

When you're used to eating meat every day, it can be hard to imagine what breakfast would look like without bacon.

Or lunch without deli meats. Or dinner without a pork chop or a chicken breast. But the world of vegetarian food is wide and tasty. Here's what a week of going veg might include. (You can find a list of helpful cookbooks on page 47.)

If you decide to give it a try, you might choose to write down what you eat in a week. How did you enjoy your meals? Note how you felt at the end of the week. **Could you keep eating like this all the time?**

	MONDAY	TUESDAY	WEDNESDAY
BREAKFAST	A bowl of cereal with dried fruits and nuts, topped with milk or soy milk.	Eggs your style with fruit and toast on the side.	Yogurt parfait with granola, frozen fruit, and honey.
LUNCH	Black bean quesadillas topped with lettuce, tomatoes, and cheese.	Pasta salad with broccoli, olives, frozen corn, carrots, and dressing.	Pan-fried tofu fingers with a cabbage coleslaw on the side.
SNACK	Home-popped popcorn.	Fruit smoothie.	Cheese and crackers.
DINNER	Pasta with tomato sauce and crumbled tofu, and a side salad sprinkled with seeds.	Quinoa and vegetable stir-fry with tempeh and peanuts.	Quick homemade lentil soup with buttered toast on the side.

THURSDAY	FRIDAY	SATURDAY	SUNDAY
Peanut, nut, or seed butter on toast and a fruit smoothie.	Oatmeal topped with nuts and drizzled with honey.	Homemade pancakes or waffles with fresh fruit and syrup.	Fried eggs and potato hash.
Leftover lentil soup with a cheese sandwich.	Hummus and pita with carrot and celery sticks.	Grilled cheese sandwich with fig jam or red pepper jelly for pizzazz.	Vegetarian pot stickers and a salad tossed with sesame dressing.
Veggies and dip.	Homemade trail mix.	A bowl of cereal! Your homemade granola?	Homemade muffin.
Veggie burgers made from beans or lentils.	Pita pizzas! Top with cheese and your choice of veggies.	Coconut chickpea curry and rice with cucumber-and-yogurt salad.	Veggie chili served on rice and topped with shredded cheese.

Telling Your Friends and Family

The way you tell your family and friends that you've decided to become a vegetarian will shape the way they react to your news.

Meat-eaters sometimes take offense or react defensively when they hear someone is a vegetarian. Some people might feel insulted if they think you're suggesting their food is not good in some way. Others may think you see them as bad people for continuing to eat meat after you've made this big decision. The important thing to stress when you tell people your news is that it's about you, not them. Becoming vegetarian is a personal choice.

PREPARING TO SHARE THE NEWS

- Think about why you want to be a vegetarian and share your reasons. Provide well-researched evidence to support your case. (You might want to show friends and family this book to prove you've done your homework!)

- Communicate to your family that you know you must eat a well-balanced diet.

- Make sure you offer to be involved in all stages of meal preparation, from planning and shopping to cooking and cleaning up. If no one else in your family is a vegetarian, the news that you want to become one can cause panic. It means more work for whoever cooks!

- Think about how you can still be involved in special meals regardless of your food choices. Some families have recipes that have been passed down through generations. They often feature meat. For example, telling your grandmother who loves to make homemade sausages that you are now a vegetarian might make her sad. Ask her if she'll help you learn another family dish that doesn't include meat.

- Figure out what dishes you can all enjoy together. Maybe the rest of your family will want to try out new recipes with you. Offer to cook dinner when you can. Try to include in your vegetarian meal something that everyone likes.

Flexible Meals Fit Everyone's Tastes

Some meals are perfect for vegetarians and non-vegetarians to enjoy together. Tacos and burritos can easily be assembled to suit individual tastes. Just add black beans to the choice of toppings for those skipping the meat. Veggie stir-fries, too, can easily satisfy meat-eaters. You can stir-fry some chicken or pork on the side for anybody who'd like to add meat to his or her portion. Pasta sauces are a snap to make flexible, too. Cook some bacon on the side, and die-hard meat-eaters can crumble it on top if they wish.

Tips from Kid Vegetarians

Trying something new can often be scary. It can help to know what to expect.

Meet five kids who are vegetarian or vegan and see what it's like from their seat at the table.

SASKIA, twelve years old

TORONTO, ONTARIO

Saskia's parents say that when she was around two years old, she was singing a song about how Mary had a little lamb—for dinner. Saskia remembers thinking that it wasn't very funny to eat a lamb because the animal wouldn't like it. Ever since then, she hasn't eaten meat. How did her parents feel? "They decided to support my decision," she says.

For Saskia, the hardest thing about being a vegetarian is following a healthy diet. But she eats a lot of beans and chickpeas and cheese. "I'm addicted to cheese," she says. One challenge she's faced is that people often believe vegetarians eat fish. That can cause confusion when she goes out.

Saskia says: "If you want to be vegetarian, you should totally go for it. It is hard, but I feel it is worth it. I love animals and I hate that they are being bred for meat."

KEELIN, eleven years old, and ROWAN, ten years old

FREDERICTON, NEW BRUNSWICK

Rowan, Keelin, and their parents are vegan. They don't eat any meat or dairy or eggs. When anyone asks Rowan why, he explains that he has always been a vegan. "That's what I was born," he says.

If you are vegan, you can't always eat the food at birthday parties, where pizza and cake rule. Vegans can't eat the cheese on a typical pizza or the eggs in a typical cake. So Rowan and Keelin eat before leaving the house and make sure to bring their own vegan cupcakes, made without eggs or butter. Sometimes other kids wonder what they've packed in their lunches. But that doesn't bother Keelin. "If anyone tries to judge you, ignore them," she says.

FAATIMAH, seven years old, YUSEF, nine years old, and FURQAN, eleven years old

DETROIT, MICHIGAN

Faatimah, Yusef, and Furqan belong to the Nation of Islam, a religious movement in the United States that promotes vegetarianism. They don't mind being different from the other kids in their school, even when kids sometimes make comments about what they bring for lunch. "They judge how the food looks because they've never tasted it before," says Faatimah. "If they tasted it, they'd say, 'Yum, this is good!'" Faatimah and her brothers love the food their mom cooks—like nachos for dinner on Fridays and broccoli burgers. A special Nation of Islam dessert called bean pie is Faatimah's favorite.

CONCLUSION:
Set the Table
for Everyone

When my extended family has dinner together, it's pretty complicated.

My sister is allergic to shrimp and fish. My mom has celiac disease, which means she can't eat wheat and a few other grains. There are nut allergies in the mix, too. Some of us don't eat garlic. Others don't eat pork for religious reasons. I prefer not to eat any kind of meat raised on a factory farm. Oh, and then there's the flexitarian, who prefers not to eat red meat.

And dinner can get even more complicated because my parents raise their own cows and butcher them to feed the family. This is a big deal. Not because we slaughter them ourselves—I've only ever helped to kill that chicken—but because we all understand that the roast or the steak or the hamburger on the table came from a real live animal that we watched grow from a baby. That makes me pause. To be honest, I don't always want to eat the beef.

What can you take away from our family dinners? There's always room for everyone—and their food preferences and restrictions—at our table. Planning a menu that works for all of us just requires thinking creatively about what to make.

Also, someone's diet is personal. You can choose to eat meat or not. Just think about why you've made your decision to eat the way you do. There are all sorts of reasons that could push you in one direction or the other. Health. Religion. Environmental concerns. Ethics. Taste.

What you eat says a lot about who you are and what you think is important. So whether you choose to eat meat or do without—to be a vegetarian or a flexitarian or a straight-up carnivore—think about why you've made that very personal decision. It's your choice.

And then, no matter what, make sure there's room at your table for everyone.

GLOSSARY

amino acids: Your body needs amino acids to work properly. They are compounds that contain elements like carbon and nitrogen and are found in some foods.

carbon dioxide: A colorless, odorless gas found naturally in the atmosphere; carbon dioxide is also added to the atmosphere by human activities such as burning fossil fuels, wood, and garbage.

cellulose: This substance helps to make up the cell walls of plants. Humans can't digest cellulose, but a cow can.

environmental cost: This is a way of measuring the total impact that a food's production has on the environment. One way to measure the environmental cost of your food is by adding up all the resources it takes to produce it.

feed conversion ratio: This is a way of stating how many pounds or kilograms of feed an animal needs to eat in order to produce one pound or kilogram of meat for people to eat.

fermentation: A process that uses bacteria to convert the sugars in foods to acids, which helps preserve the food and adds to its nutritional value.

flexitarian: A word that describes someone who chooses to eat less meat than most meat-eaters but is not a full vegetarian.

food security: You have food security when you can access enough healthy, affordable food. A country has food security when the government can be sure that everyone who lives there has access to healthy, affordable food.

fossil fuel: A carbon-rich fuel such as gasoline or coal that was formed millions of years ago when prehistoric plants and animals decayed.

greenhouse gas: A term that describes heat-trapping gases such as methane and carbon dioxide that are building up in the Earth's atmosphere and causing climate change.

hunter-gatherer: A person who doesn't rely on farming for food but rather collects and hunts everything that he or she eats.

industrial farm: A term for large farms that produce huge quantities of one type of food. They tend to use more resources and have a greater impact on the environment than smaller farms. Another term for this is "factory farm."

legume: A legume is a food that grows in the pods of certain plants. Examples include chickpeas and lentils.

methane: This is a powerful greenhouse gas that cows and other ruminants belch. It contributes to climate change.

micronutrient deficiency: This is the name for a condition that people develop when they don't get enough nutrition from their food. Even though they aren't hungry and feel like they have enough food, their bodies are lacking certain essential nutrients, such as iron, vitamin A, and zinc.

nutrient: Nutrients are substances that help your body grow, function properly, and stay healthy. They are found in your food.

pescatarian: A word that describes someone who doesn't eat meat but does eat fish.

protein: An important nutrient that your body needs to make and maintain your bones, organs, blood, and muscles.

ruminant: A category of grass-eating mammals that have four compartments in their stomachs for digesting grasses and other tough plants. Ruminants include cows, sheep, and deer.

vegan: A word for someone who doesn't eat anything that comes from an animal, including eggs, dairy products, honey, and meat.

SOURCES

In addition to interviews with experts, these are some of the sources that author Sarah Elton consulted in her research for this book.

Food and Agriculture Organization of the United Nations. "Edible Insects: Future Prospects for Food and Feed Security." Rome, 2013. Online.

Food and Agriculture Organization of the United Nations. "Livestock's Long Shadow: Environmental Issues and Options." Rome, 2006. Online.

Intergovernmental Panel on Climate Change. Various reports. Online.

John Hopkins Center for a Livable Future. "Industrial Food Animal Production in America: Examining the Impact of the Pew Commission's Priority Recommendations." Online.

The Pew Charitable Trusts. "Big Chicken: Pollution and Industrial Chicken Production in America." Online.

The Pew Charitable Trusts. Reforming Industrial Animal Agriculture Project. Reports, articles, and fact sheets. Online.

Pollan, Michael. *Food Rules: An Eater's Manual.* New York: Penguin Books, 2009.

Pollan, Michael. *The Omnivore's Dilemma.* New York: The Penguin Press, 2006.

Safran Foer, Jonathan. *Eating Animals.* New York: Back Bay Books, 2010.

Spencer, Colin. *Vegetarianism: A History.* London: Grub Street Publishing, 2016.

Stuart, Tristram. *Bloodless Revolution: A Cultural History of Vegetarianism from 1600 to Modern Times.* New York: W. W. Norton & Company, 2006.

FURTHER READING

To learn more about food choices and their impact on you and the planet, check out these books and online resources.

Carolan, Michael. *The Real Cost of Cheap Food.* New York: Earthscan, 2011.

Curtis, Andrea, and Nick Saul. *The Stop: How the Fight for Good Food Transformed a Community and Inspired a Movement.* Toronto: Random House Canada, 2013.

Elton, Sarah. *Consumed: Food for a Finite Planet.* Chicago: University of Chicago Press, 2013.

Elton, Sarah. *Locavore: From Farmers' Fields to Rooftop Gardens—How Canadians Are Changing the Way We Eat.* Toronto: HarperCollins, 2011.

Elton, Sarah. *Starting from Scratch: What You Should Know about Food and Cooking.* Toronto: OwlKids Books, 2014.

Environmental Working Group. "Meat Eater's Guide to Climate Change + Health." Online.

Johnson, Lorraine. *City Farmer: Adventures in Urban Food Growing.* Vancouver: Greystone Books, 2010.

Kingsolver, Barbara. *Animal, Vegetable, Miracle: Our Year of Seasonal Eating.* New York: HarperCollins, 2007.

Patel, Raj. *Stuffed and Starved: Markets, Power and the Hidden Battle for the World's Food System.* 2nd ed. New York: Melville House, 2012.

World Wildlife Fund. Environmental Footprint Calculator. Online.

RECOMMENDED VEGETARIAN COOKBOOKS

You can find great recipes in these kid-friendly vegetarian cookbooks.

Bittman, Mark. *How to Cook Everything Vegetarian: Simple Meatless Recipes for Great Food.* Hoboken, NJ: John Wiley & Sons, Inc., 2007.

Cronish, Nettie. *Everyday Flexitarian: Recipes for Vegetarians and Meat Lovers Alike.* Vancouver: Whitecap Books, 2011.

Fearnley-Whittingstall, Hugh. *River Cottage Veg: 200 Inspired Vegetable Recipes.* Toronto: Random House Canada, 2011.

Katzen, Molly. *Honest Pretzels: And 64 Other Amazing Recipes for Cooks Ages 8 & Up.* Berkley, CA: Tricycle Press, 2009.

ACKNOWLEDGMENTS

Thank you to historians Dr. Lesley Abrams of Oxford University and Dr. Jayeeta Sharma of the University of Toronto, Scarborough.

FOOD FOR THOUGHT

"Animals are my friends...
and I don't eat my friends."

—GEORGE BERNARD SHAW,
playwright

"My favorite animal is steak."

—FRAN LEBOWITZ,
photographer

"You can judge a man's true
character by the way he treats
his fellow animals."

—PAUL McCARTNEY,
musician

"Eat food. Not too much.
Mostly plants."

—MICHAEL POLLAN,
author and journalist

"There is no fundamental
difference between man and
animals in their ability to feel
pleasure and pain, happiness,
and misery."

—CHARLES DARWIN,
scientist

"By eating meat we share
the responsibility of climate
change, the destruction of our
forests, and the poisoning of
our air and water. The simple
act of becoming a vegetarian
will make a difference in the
health of our planet. If you're
not able to entirely stop
eating meat, you can still
decide to make an effort to
cut back."

—THICH NHAT HANH,
spiritual leader and author

"I did not become a
vegetarian for my health,
I did it for the health of
the chickens."

—ISAAC BASHEVIS SINGER,
author

"This is my invariable advice
to people: Learn how to
cook—try new recipes,
learn from your mistakes,
be fearless, and above all
have fun!"

—JULIA CHILD,
chef and author